Terry Tucker

The Last COIN Lecture

GRIN Verlag

Bibliografische Information der Deutschen Nationalbibliothek:

Die Deutsche Bibliothek verzeichnet diese Publikation in der Deutschen National-
bibliografie; detaillierte bibliografische Daten sind im Internet über http://dnb.d-
nb.de/ abrufbar.

Imprint:

Copyright © 2011 GRIN Verlag GmbH
Druck und Bindung: Books on Demand GmbH, Norderstedt Germany
ISBN: 978-3-640-80592-1

This book at GRIN:

http://www.grin.com/en/e-book/165140/the-last-coin-lecture

GRIN - Your knowledge has value

Der GRIN Verlag publiziert seit 1998 wissenschaftliche Arbeiten von Studenten, Hochschullehrern und anderen Akademikern als eBook und gedrucktes Buch. Die Verlagswebsite www.grin.com ist die ideale Plattform zur Veröffentlichung von Hausarbeiten, Abschlussarbeiten, wissenschaftlichen Aufsätzen, Dissertationen und Fachbüchern.

Visit us on the internet:

http://www.grin.com/

http://www.facebook.com/grincom

http://www.twitter.com/grin_com

The Last COIN Lecture

This is my last lecture at the counterinsurgency training center here in Kabul; I am humbled, deeply humbled and honored to have had the privilege of working with such a fine team; you have taught me much and my hope is that I was able to impart some small measure to you as well.

Science, History and Art all have something in common: they all depend on metaphor, on the recognition of patterns, and the realization that something is like something else to focus attention on a vantage point. On where we have been.
We only know our future by the past we project into it; in a sense our history is all we have.

Lets briefly explore this sense of history with an example:

I would like to begin with a brief look at the war; Many Americans opposed it, Europe was hostile to the idea as well, conventional operations were generally speaking successful, but it was clear that post-conflict or phase IV operations was a catastrophe, an enemy defeated in battle resumed resistance after his army had been shattered.
We do not need to rehash the amount of violence and misery. But in retrospect was our effort at social engineering despite our best intentions, simply impossible to attempt or a failure of good execution? In retrospect, of course the real central theme is Good idea impossible to achieve or Good idea badly executed?
This example is critical for it describes the US Civil War; for how the political elements are inextricably tied to the social and economic elements and failing to understanding the past is as important to understanding the present and the future.

There is a broader historical context but it is also clearly more than just the broader historical context as COIN does not always easily lend itself to rapid tactical learning.

Additionally a survey of US doctrinal manuals and publication dates provides clues that our true focus after WW II was guerrilla and counter-guerrilla operations and not COIN. For example: following WW II it was FM 31-20, *Operations against Guerilla Forces*, dated 1951; ten years later it was FM 31-15, *Operations against Irregular Forces; by 1963 doctrine had morphed into two manual – Counter Guerrilla Operations and* US Counterinsurgency Force; *by 1990 it was Military Operations in Low Intensity Conflict* with a heavy emphasis on light forces in Full Spectrum Operations.

In essence, with perfect hindsight, it might beg the question: regarding counterinsurgency, where has been our frame of reference and focus been on?

The military instrument is only one portion of the overall COIN effort.

We seem to have trouble with identifying continuity with the past as revolutions, small wars and insurrections seem to be treated more as an episode in time than a kind of war. Even strategy treated as a idea with a continuous history is interesting but the results of success seem to be only just more plausible than definitive, while failure becomes an object lesson in what not to do. What we have with doctrine is a set of principles learned from history; and with these principles we expect to project into the future and to predict some measure of success.

For instance, consider the following historical tenets: the political nature of insurgency and counterinsurgency defies codification; it is difficult to understand the relationship between political and military action, the public is critical of operations, and a multinational coalition must act with unity of purpose and unity of command; and while these historical principles have proven valid over time this appears to be an unprecedented challenge to the current coalition.

The whole of government or comprehensive and integrated approach is not new; one only needs to think of Gwynn, Roosevelt, Churchill, Thompson and Kitson. Achieving this integration though is problematic as one considers how best to integrate and leverage resources such as UNAMA, the World Bank, the World Health Organization, US Aid and a host of agencies that are operating in your operating environment.

If the short of it is that we must engage the population, win its support and whoever does this first wins the battle then how does one win the next village, district, province and war? How does this link and synch with the problem set identification tasks of decide, detect, deliver and assess?

What are we assessing when the legacy of our collective processes in IPB, and MDMP was developed over 25 years ago? The new Imperative for the Counterinsurgent and perhaps for the 21st Century is the ability to see what is not there.

If the use of acronym tools such as ASCOPE-PMESII and DIME, taken together as part of this collective process equate to knowledge of hard power and soft power how does one then translate that to *smart power, to a strategy* in a comprehensive and integrated approach? Once again, if the population is the center of gravity in a COIN fight then its religion and culture are the populations' center of gravity, is this where in lies the elements of smart power? What does this mean? The New imperative associated with this transformation to "Smart Power", our ability to see what is not there is directly related to the emergence of more effective ways to detect the absence of a piece of knowledge; In essence it is the search for "Absence Detection" Absence detection is what we all do when we search for information. Identifying what is absent by observation is inherently difficult. The very idea runs counter to the idea; that absence of evidence sometimes is evidence of absence. This can be obvious: What makes you think there's no elephant in your room?

IN ESSENCE , IN COIN, WHAT YOU DON'T KNOW CAN HURT YOU, EVEN KILL YOU.

By way of a related example, some terms used to describe non-conventional warfare might include: partisan warfare, irregular warfare, rebellion, peasant wars, guerrilla war, revolutionary war, low intensity conflict, and fourth general war.

One has difficulty understanding if these terms are viewed as expressions of intellectual fashion or describe a country specific conflict. It seems that the term counterinsurgency is neither understood as a "hearts and minds" approach nor associated with the complexity of the social dynamics.

Once again, following a loose logic, if the approach is to assume that the population is the prize, the center of gravity, then by implication counterinsurgency is about maintaining, extending or initiating "social order" and I meant that in as many a sense as you think it to be.

One may argue that there is large difference between an insurgency, and, say, a rebellion or a peasant revolt but perhaps this difference is a fallacy because either way one is seeking a new social order; political, social and economic order. It is the level of available resources that determines the peasants' a.k.a insurgent's tactics and strategy.

On a larger scale the social unrest in Europe between 1300's and 1600's were fought to change political, social and economic elements of society. In this regard, England's intervention in Savoy in 1655 takes on a different historical context, as well as might the intervention in Syria-Lebanon in the 1860's, the era of Bloody Kansas and the era of Reconstruction.

So, with the wrong metaphor the wrong lessons have dangerous implications.

Doctrine therefore is a general framework and any notion or suggestion of predictability, scalability or replication should be viewed with suspicion.

Although the underlying theory of war does not change and of which insurgency and counterinsurgency are a complex sub set; the form, scope and consequences do. We are oft reminded that those that fail to study history are doomed to repeat it. In this sense COIN has failed as equally as it has succeeded – replete with lessons learned the hard way and the myriad principles and theory misapplied.

Over the last several years insurgency and counterinsurgency has not enjoyed such popularity since the Kennedy administration. Hubert Humphrey expressed this when he spoke of this bold new type of warfare and aggression, which would rank with the discovery of gunpowder as constituting the most significant threat to a State's security.

In essence, by inference and implication this popularity in this new-old type of warfare symbolizes the progressive severance of traditional social and economic links, the erosion of governance and a moral explosion and polarization of the disenfranchised and the disinherited. Insurgency as a form of warfare constitutes mans supreme challenge to the awesome power of machines and technology. Algeria, Vietnam and Russian Afghanistan are cases in point: they engaged the most advanced war machines of the time and defeated the presumption of technology.

America's interest in insurgency/counterinsurgency in the 60's was primarily one of a defensive nature; loses in China, Cuba, Laos, and Vietnam is cases in point. As a result, thus, have we become more attracted to the myths and methods of insurgency and counterinsurgency than to understanding the causes, root causes' of these type wars?

Besides our vague understanding of how social order and all its elements is critical to COIN doctrine and strategy, we have routinely approached this fact with the simple idea that the simple task of the insurgent is to destroy while that of the counterinsurgent is to build and protect. But this is to disregard not only the lessons of history, but contemporary lessons in Afghanistan as well.

The insurgent does not simply seek to destroy his enemy and to inflict loss, but to delegitimize the government and to establish rival governance and systems through the establishment of parallel hierarchies because even in its clandestine state; even in the lack of official presence, the shadow governance must prove its efficacy; for instance, China, Vietnam , Algeria and the Mexican Revolution were all different insurgencies yet the commonality in history is how the insurgents were able to exploit and establish key principles to establish effective shadow governance and how ineffective government responses exacerbated the problem.

In essence the enemies' task is to use selective violence but if not more importantly his task is to "Out Administer", not out fight his enemy.

Therefore the conditions of insurgency as defined by current doctrine as the pre-requisites of an insurgency are not entirely created by the violence, the conspiracy, or disinformation, but are already partially inherent in the cultural and social structure; in essence the social order. Additionally, external sanctuary as both an extension of social order and a dynamic of an insurgency is of far greater psychological and diplomatic value than just the political or military value.

In essence the organizers of an insurgency place far more emphasis on the "human factors"; they exploit a triple dislocation of the PMESII variables that the military alone is incapable of countering alone; primarily the political, social and economic elements. *Politically* it is the dislocation of traditional authority; an increasing freedom from domination by foreigners; *socially* it is characterized by the emergence of entire new classes of societies in the form of displaced persons, urban workers, gaps in generational views and classes as the young, the marginalized and disinherited reject either the old, the new or the existing, and, economically by the demand and unequal distribution of economic development. The question to ask is: *Where is the distribution of poverty and austerity as opposed to the distribution of wealth*? These pressures led to direct and indirect confrontation with those that would adhere to or prefer to maintain the cultural, political and economic status quo: in essence the social order.

Current doctrine is premised on hearts and minds, carrots and sticks and transformation; fundamentally this is social and cultural re-engineering. The keystone concept in this doctrine; a keystone not completely understood is the development of "social capital". The building of networks of trust that use the components' of social capital, because to achieve moral and political isolation of the enemy requires not only a severance, a cutting of the old but also the forging of new links. As the French so aptly describe it: it is to *legislate in the void.*

The insurgent legislates this void in the social order by establishing the new, sometimes even creating the new, while maintaining congruence with the old. He exploits the distribution of poverty, he legislates in the void by providing key governance and social leadership tied to the existing cultural and social base; the primacy of politics at the local level is demonstrated by the fact that prime attention is paid to the human and social dynamics – the human factor's of war.   Seeing what is not there is critical to understanding the social order.

For instance, What if measures of effectiveness such as shipping costs, smuggling rates and absentee land ownership provided the clues to the relationship and similarities of the perceived and simultaneous effectiveness of security, governance and development? Of the social order, the human factors? How do you separate behavior toward policies and actions from ones feelings and attitudes?

In conclusion, it is more than the cliff notes of history and historical context that should shape our potential planning and responses. Words, metaphor and the appropriate context in sum equate to both cognitive effect and planning and problem set identification effect.

Words and context does matter heavily and the very term counterinsurgency fails to adequately describe the type of conflict that one is really engaged in. It fails to denote the conventional, the civil, the punitive, the militarist, the civil-military, the cultural, the social, the enabling concepts, or the comprehensive and integrated approach.

It seems to treat the problem as one that is more administrative, managerial and technical in the solution and It appears to be more concerned with procedural approaches than substantive ones. It seems to denote a direct action kinetic approach with less consideration for the important considerations of the political, economic and social elements in which the social order exists or is established and out administering is infinitely more important that out fighting ones enemy.